CAMP CHRONICLES

BY

MILDRED PHELPS STOKES HOOKER

WITH INTRODUCTION AND NOTES BY
PAUL F. JAMIESON

AFTERWORD BY WHITELAW REID

ADIRONDACK MUSEUM
BLUE MOUNTAIN LAKE, NEW YORK

Library of Congress Catalogue Card No. 64-24123
ISBN 0-910020-16-7

Printed by Queen City Printers Inc., Burlington, VT 05401

CAMP CHRONICLES

Upper St. Regis Lake and St. Regis Mountain

I N T R O D U C T I O N

AN UNUSUAL CHRISTMAS card reached ninety-five people in the mails of December, 1952. It was a small printed book with nineteen photographs pasted in. On the cover, taking the place of a title, was the view of an Adirondack lake with a sail in the midst and a mountain as backdrop. On opening the wrapper, the ninety-five recognized the lake as Upper St. Regis, for nearly all were the summer neighbors of the author in the camp-colony on that lake and on Spitfire. The book was addressed to them. The title page bore the letters "Camp Chronicles" but no by-line, for the author wrote a personal message, with her signature, on the flyleaf of each copy.

It is natural to speak of this book in the past tense. The author herself has only one copy left of the five she reserved from the private printing of one hundred in 1952. Librarians and private collectors find their efforts balked by a closed circle of St. Regisites. The original recipients will not part with a book so intimately linked with their summer lives and leisure. Though it is listed in *Adirondack Bibliography,* few outsiders have had access to the book or even know of its existence. At Dr. Francis Trudeau's request a copy was given to the Saranac Lake Free Library. The library of St. Lawrence University recently acquired a copy following the death of an original owner. And the Adirondack Museum has one. So far as is known, these three are the only copies held in collections open to the public.

My acquaintance with *Camp Chronicles* came while I was compiling an anthology of the Adirondacks. Mrs. Hooker's book, I felt, is more than a charming family story. It is local history of a bright era in the north-central Adirondacks—the days of Paul Smith and Dr. E. L. Trudeau. It is the record of a summer colony unique in many ways but typical of the Adirondacks in the tendency of the family camp to spread into a small village of cabins, each unit with a separate function. And the book has bearings on the national scene of the last eighty years. Here is a group of representative Americans who brought to their play the same energy, high spirits, and resourcefulness that in their working days made the nation a world power.

The author's claim in the opening sentence to be the longest inhabitant of the Upper St. Regis camps has been strengthened by the passing of twelve years. This summer (1963) she is spending her eightieth season in camp. When she first came in 1883, she was just two years old—the second youngest of the nine children of Anson Phelps Stokes, New York banker.

By 1890 Paul Smith, "the genial proprietor," as Mrs. Hooker calls him, was filled with astonishment and pride at the community then flourishing in the neighborhood of his hotel and landholdings. A contributor to *Forest and Stream* quotes him: "I never saw anything like it! There's not a foot of land on that lake for sale this minute, and there's not a man in it but what's a millionaire, and some of them ten times over"; then, after mentioning the Stokeses, the Reids, and some of their neighbors, "I tell you if there's a spot on the face of the earth where millionaires go to play at house keeping in log cabins and tents as they do here I have it yet to hear about."

Today the colony of about forty camps on the two lakes forms a little world of relative timelessness amidst twentieth-century change. Descendants of some of the original lease-holders and owners come back summer after summer. Young and old mingle as in the eighties. Mrs. Hooker and her generation are now passing the camp traditions on to their grandchildren and great-grandchildren. The hymn sings that originated in the last century are still held, not on Birch Island now but at Camp Red Pines, which Mrs. Hooker shares with her son-in-law and daughter, the Dyson Duncans. The telephone, electricity, plumbing, and central marketing have come, but the log cabins and general "campiness" remain. In many camps one still walks from the sitting room to the dining room on a carpet of pine needles, kicking the cones aside. Motorboats, to be sure, have largely replaced rowboats. But the sailboat has kept its dominant place. Each generation eagerly learns from its seniors the skills of racing in the light, variable winds of narrow St. Regis waters. At most hours of the day the two lakes are gay and ceremonious with the sails and signal flags of the members of the St. Regis Yacht Club, which had its formal beginning in 1897 and its informal one still earlier in the races to church.

There is no trace of nostalgia in Mrs. Hooker's memories. Through the genius of the place and an art of her own, she has achieved that enviable condition where memories and present realities do not jar but enrich each other.

The book is reprinted here substantially as it was written in 1952. Most of the illustrations are reproductions of family photos taken in the eighties by Mrs. Hooker's mother, with an old-style camera and wet plates. Several have been added to those in the original edition.

PAUL F. JAMIESON

vii

F O R E W O R D

WHEN THIS little book was first issued twelve years ago, it was intended only for my friends and neighbors on the lakes. Now that it seems destined to be seen by others, a few words of elucidation seem to be in order.

The "Ransom" of the chronicles was my husband, Dr. Ransom Spafard Hooker. The "Louis" was my cousin Louis Slade. His camp is not mentioned in the listing because he and his wife were no longer alive when the book was distributed, and their camp was vacant. The list given comprised only the names of the original owners of the camps still in active use. The names in parentheses denoted the family or families living on these camp sites in 1952. No attempt was made to list the many people who had owned or rented the camps in the interim. This meant leaving out the names of many well-known people who were camp owners.

I made no mention either of the many interesting guests who were visitors here. They ranged from the Governor-General of Canada and his suite and General Marshall to senators, ambassadors and other distinguished foreigners, bishops, literary men, and artists, the latter including Maxfield Parrish, Sergeant Kendall, and Hamilton King. Alice Roosevelt, President "Teddy's" daughter, was a frequent guest at the Hammond camp while it was rented by James Roosevelt.

The years have been good to our lakes. They have not lost their beauty. Nor have they lost their charm and appeal. Six more grandchildren of the original campers now own their own places and others have joined us too, so that practically all the camps are now occupied.

MILDRED PHELPS STOKES HOOKER

CAMP CHRONICLES

It will be seventy years this summer since I first came to camp as a little girl of two, so I think I can fairly claim to be the longest, if not the oldest, inhabitant.

In 1876, five years before I was born, Father brought his family to Paul Smith's and went into rough camp with them on what we later called Birch Island.

They slept on balsam branches and washed in the lake, and used their only pillow, so I have been told, as a bed for my sister Ethel, who was then a baby. But though they lived in such primitive fashion and did without so many other things, they showed that they had the proper St. Regis spirit by immediately building, to quote my father, "what was said to be the first sailboat ever seen in this neighborhood—a catamaran made by fastening together two rowboats by a platform and placing a centerboard in the platform."

Father was so charmed by the beauty and peace of the Upper Lake—there were no camps at all on it then—that he bought the island from a Mr. Norton for $200.

They all loved it here, so it was natural that, when some years later the doctor advised a summer in the Adirondacks, they should decide to come back. (The doctor, by the way, was Dr. Loomis,[1] who only a year before had told Dr. Trudeau, who was trying to interest him in Koch's discoveries, that he "didn't believe much in germs." Dr. Trudeau had converted him in the interim.)

Newton and Sadie were neither of them strong and Mother was expecting a baby. To rough it as they had before seemed hardly advisable, so they decided to put up a more permanent camp. Father also decided to look more carefully into his title, and finding that the Mutual Life Company claimed some rights under a mortgage, he paid them $500 and got a deed from them too. I have often heard him say that it was cheaper to pay them than to hire a lawyer to prove that he didn't have to.

Those of us who motor up nowadays in station wagons overflowing with children, dogs, and other accessories look upon the trip to camp as quite an undertaking, but listen to Mother's description of that family expedition in 1883:

"Busy packing all the morning, Patrick left in afternoon with horses, Muggins and Sport [a pug and a setter], and a truck load of freight. Papa chartered what they call a special parlor horse car direct from 42nd Street to Ausable for $100, and we take in it our horses, carriage, all camping outfits, extra trunks, stores, etc. They go to Plattsburg and arrive tomorrow evening. Then to Ausable where the freight will be taken off by wagons to Paul Smith's." She then proceeds to list "baggage, etc., for summer campaign of the Stokes family."

"Anson Phelps Stokes, wife, seven children, one niece (Mabel Slade), about ten servants, Miss Rondell, one coachman, three horses, two dogs, one carriage, five large boxes of tents, three cases of wine, two packages of stovepipe, two stoves, one bale china, one iron pot, four washstands, one barrel of hardware,

2

four bundles of poles, seventeen cots and seventeen mattresses, four canvas packages, one buckboard, five barrels, one-half barrel, two tubs of butter, one bag coffee, one chest tea, one crate china, twelve rugs, four milkcans, two drawing boards, twenty-five trunks, thirteen small boxes, one boat, one hamper."

Apropos of the "three cases of wine," many years later my brother Anson and I were sunning ourselves on the breakwater when a guide rowed by with some sightseers from the hotel. We heard him tell them that Father had four sons "who ain't one of them never touched a drop," and wondered if it were our duty to row out and disabuse them.

Paul Smith's Hotel

There is a Paul Smith story always linked in my mind with this one. Paul was talking about the family to a man who had been visiting us and exclaimed, "Just think, nine children and not a damn bad one in the lot." Mother thought it a wonderful compliment.

I don't, of course, remember Paul Smith in the very earliest days. When I knew him he was the genial proprietor of the hotel with a fund of amusing anecdotes, but before that he was, as most of you know, a hunting guide who "guided" many well-known men, including Mr. Rockefeller and Mr. Harriman; Dr. Trudeau did know him earlier and pictures him "in the center of the little dining room, after having put out his hounds in the morning hunt, beaming with good nature and standing in his shirt sleeves with four or five dog chains still slung over his shoulders, carving venison or roast for his guests and joking with everybody around."

Paul Smith never put on any airs even after he became a millionaire, and his son Phelps was like him. At the time of the First World War there was a camp owner on Osgood who was supposed to be more intimate than she should have been with Count von Bernstorff when he was German ambassador. Rumors were rife about secret meetings and hidden wires and messages to Germany. She owed Phelps Smith a good deal of money, and being pressed to pay, at last agreed to give him a cheque if he wouldn't cash it until later. The cheque was cashed the next day, and the irate debtor arrived in high dudgeon at the hotel. "How could you!" she stormed. "We had a gentleman's agreement about that cheque!" "Well, now," said Phelps, "I never did claim to be no gentleman and I never supposed you were no lady."

To return to the summer of 1883. After a night in the train, breakfast in Plattsburg and a further train trip to Ausable, they took a "rockaway, a buckboard and another carriage" for the thirty-six mile drive to Paul Smith's, "stopping by the roadside several times to heat the baby's milk." I was that baby and am mortified to think that I wanted a bottle when I was two years old!

They didn't arrive at Paul's till late, so had to spend the night there before rowing up to the island to pick out the best camp site. Father and Mother had a hard time choosing between the southwesterly and northwesterly ends of the island. They didn't realize then that eventually the camp would spread until it included both.

They spent some days at the hotel while preliminary work was being done.

Dr. Trudeau in his autobiography describes Paul Smith's as "a rough and remote place, very different from what it has become in these days of Pullman trains, automobiles, speed launches and parlor camps. Things were very primitive but most comfortable. There was no running water in the hotel, and a trip to the spring under the bank with a pail supplied the drinking water; but Mrs. Paul Smith's influence was seen everywhere in the house, in the clean and comfortable rooms, the good beds, the excellent cooking which she did or supervised herself, and the feeling of welcome and home with which she impressed all her guests." He adds that at that time "Paul Smith's was only a sporting hostelry, the resort of hunters and fishermen, and few ladies, and no children, were ever seen among the guests." But this was when he first came there some ten years earlier. By the time our family came, ladies and children were no longer a rarity. In fact, by 1875 Dr. Trudeau's own family had come there with him.

Mother speaks of walking from the hotel to the little church of St. John's in the Wilderness. This was the little log church which we all loved so much, which burned down in 1927.

We can be grateful to Dr. Trudeau for our church as well as for so many other things. During their first winter at the hotel, he and Mrs. Trudeau had greatly missed church, and he worried so much because there were no services available to the guides and their families that he himself held a Sunday school in the little school house on the road to Bloomingdale so as to do something, to quote his own words, "to carry the blessed message to those

The Little Log Church

children who had so little opportunity to hear it."

For a while services were held occasionally in the hotel parlors, but by the fall of 1876 Dr. Trudeau had started a subscription list for "a little log chapel," and Mrs. Louis Livingston, who was one of those he appealed to, got him off to a good start by giving a fair in her New York home which brought in fourteen hundred dollars. Paul Smith gave the land and logs.

The little chapel was consecrated by Bishop Doane on September 13, 1877. It soon outgrew its seating capacity and had to be enlarged. Again it was Dr. Trudeau who raised the necessary funds.

He was warden of the little church all his life, and how well I remember him carrying the collection plate to the altar in his fascinating high leggins with my father by his side. I think it was because Dr. Trudeau and my father always took up the collection that the custom grew up of having them sit in the two front pews. It made it easy for them to step out together.

St. John's played an important part in camp life. We were always a church-going community, and it was a gay and lovely sight on sunny Sunday mornings to see the long line of rowboats with flags fluttering at bow and stern wending its way down through the sloughs to church. Gayest of all was a boat from the Livingston camp with white paint and red cushions.

Even sailboats joined in the parade. Father used to say that though he didn't, of course, approve of Sunday racing, it was quite another matter to take two boats and see who could get to church first! He was happiest when he had the minister on board, for then he couldn't possibly be late for service; and this was a privilege he often enjoyed, for Sunday morning preachers were usually our Saturday night guests. In fact, we used to call one of our cabins The Rectory or The Prophet's Chamber because our ministers used it so often.

In those days one minister ministered to a host of little missions in the neighborhood. Mr. Larom, who held services at St. John's for years, was known as "The Bishop of All Outdoors." He did a good deal of his traveling in a canoe with a two-bladed paddle, and when he arrived early enough on Saturdays he would hoist a little sail and join in the afternoon boat race. It was really very sporting of him, for in spite of his handicap allowance, he always came in way behind everyone else. Being dependent on his own power, so to speak, there were times when bad weather or other emergencies prevented his getting there at all. But this didn't prevent our holding services. We would just dispense with the sermon and one of my brothers would step out of our pew and read the lessons.

My brothers were not the only laymen to officiate in our little church. Years later when Bishop Brent was making his annual visit to the Reids, he developed a high fever. Ransom, called in to see him, said he must stay in bed, but this the bishop refused to do on account of the services. They argued the matter up and down, neither willing to give in. At last Bishop Brent said he would stay in bed on just one condition, if Ransom would hold the services. He reluctantly agreed but stipulated that he would not be expected to preach.

This was after our log church had burned, which it did just as we had celebrated its fiftieth anniversary.

Ransom was chairman of the committee for rebuilding and wanted to build a church of logs just like the old one, but there were more, including two large subscribers, who felt that permanent material should be used, so he bowed to their wishes. I think Mr. Distin, the architect, was very successful in keeping so much of the spirit of the old church, even though stone was used instead of logs.

There was quite a question about the windows, too. Some of us wanted to use Gothic tracery and clear glass so that we could look out at the pines and Dr. Trudeau's grave, but here again the majority preferred stained glass, Mrs. Whitelaw Reid using the clinching argument that someone would surely put in stained glass someday anyway, and then it would be too late for us to make sure that they were harmonious in color and design. She quite convinced us by taking us to see a church near Purchase where enormous prophets and smaller subjects were jumbled up with flower windows from Tiffany Studios to the detriment of all.

Churchgoing entailed a walk as well as a row. We used to land at the hotel docks and walk up either by the board walk bordering the road or by the path on the other side of the "ice pond." For the very first years there was only the path, but when in no hurry we much preferred it anyway, for it led through a lovely grove of pine trees and past an Indian camp. The only trouble was that being a Sunday we weren't allowed to buy the sweet grass baskets and moccasins and little birch bark canoes that the Indians sold. However, they always made the rounds of the camps once in the season in a big boat filled with their wares, so we didn't feel too badly.

Once arrived at church, we all refreshed ourselves by drinking from the water cooler that stood in the entry. Evidently, like Dr. Loomis, we didn't believe in germs, for we all shared a single glass!

The Indians were not the only ones to make the rounds of the camps. Russ used to bring furs around once a year before he had his store in Saranac. An Englishman, who lived for some time on the mountain, used to come around and sell his pictures, and later the nuns brought beautiful embroideries. Also, for many years a distinguished-looking colored clergyman, carrying a visiting card inscribed with the impressive title of "Bishop Jones," used to come begging for money for a colored school. My brother Anson asked him how he came by his title when he belonged to a denomination that didn't have bishops. It didn't stump him at all. He replied with great dignity, "Bishop am mah first name."

On July 23rd, 1883, although camp, to quote my mother, was "not near ready," the family moved to the island. By night they had six tents ready besides the cook house and dining tent. Five beds in the "parlor" (a fourteen by fourteen tent) accommodated the overflow.

No one delivered supplies in those early days, so Mother took with her forty chickens and an old hen, "to kill as required." She describes buying the chickens from a farm woman who apologized for asking twenty cents apiece. The old hen cost twenty-five cents.

Father used to rent cows and keep them on Cow Island and later at the farm to provide his large family with milk. Cow Island was later known as Hog Island when the pigs moved in, and as

Pearl Island when it achieved the distinction of housing humans.

The farm consisted of fifty acres of mainland which Father bought, for $1.50 an acre, very shortly after buying Birch Island. That same summer he bought Pearl Island, High Island, and the two (now three) islands in front of our camp. They were listed on the deed as Chicken Coop Island and Two Tree Island.

Meat used to be sent up in barrels from New York; but this wasn't too satisfactory an arrangement, for it often spoiled in transit. Sometimes a whole lamb or a side of beef could be bought from someone up here.

The Parlor Tent

Supplies were kept in storerooms and in ice houses. The ice houses were regular cold storage plants with thick insulated walls. Every camp had one. These were filled yearly with ice from the lakes, although often some of the ice lasted for more than one season. I still remember the chill that one felt on entering them, and the feeling, amounting almost to awe, with

10

which we children gazed on the rows and rows of delectable delicacies, rising tier on tier to the roof.

How different most of those provisions were to those stocked nowadays. No packaged foods, no "ready mixes" or jellos or Aunt Jemima's. (Yeast came in a little package by mail from New York every week for a grand baking.) Many of the things were French. I remember especially the *"petits pois Mercier extra fines."* I used to plan that someday, when I was grown up, I'd have a whole can for myself. And there were French sardines and deviled chicken and prunes in glass jars. My brother Anson maintains that no other canned fruit ever tasted like the camp kind of Golden Gate Lemon Clingstone peaches, while Harold remembers especially the big boxes of macaroni. Flour and sugar were stocked in barrels, and there was always a whole chest of tea and a tub of butter.

Alas, in spite of her well-stocked storerooms, Mother wrote in 1884 that she didn't dare give a dinner party, for Charles was "so poor and always thinking he has too much to do." Father came to the rescue and sent her up another chef from New York who had "been all winter in the White House." His cooking was pronounced "delicious," so I presume they made up for lost time and invited all the neighbors in to share in their good fortune.

We relied entirely on canned vegetables. No one dreamed that some day Hobart would deliver fresh ones right at our docks and that later still there would be markets in Saranac which would supply us. There was, however, a forerunner of Hardy Sweet, a man who built a little boat shelter in the lower slough and from there rowed around with milk; and when launches came in Paul Smith decided to deliver meat from his "cooler" in a launch, and this he did for years.

Sometimes, in spite of the large camp household, which often numbered around thirty, the supplies were not all consumed by

11

the time we left. Once towards the end of the season I was driving with Mother on the road to Saranac when she noticed a dilapidated house overflowing with children. She promptly arranged with our guide, Sam Newell, that as soon as we left he was to go over at night with all that was left in the ice house and storeroom, put the things on the porch, and sneak away without being seen. I have often thought of the joy with which those poor parents must have discovered this miraculous store in the morning.

The White House Chef

Another institution at Paul Smith's much used by the campers was the store. It was kept by a man called Henry (everyone called him that, so I haven't the least idea what his last name was).

He took a great interest in his work and did it so successfully that my brother Anson says he has often referred to him in sermons as a man who, having a relatively small job, put his whole heart in it and did it to perfection.

When he had run the store for some thirty years, hardly stepping out of the door, Dr. James got up a purse among the campers to send him abroad in appreciation of his services. He was a great lover of beauty and enjoyed his trip to the fullest extent, coming home especially enthusiastic about the fine mosaics in Italy.

In early days the store was under the hotel and was reached by a flight of steps. In those days, too, the hotel was on quite a little hill, which was later dug away to make the store more accessible. Many of the fine trees around the place were unfortunately cut down at the same time as a precaution against forest fires, which had on more than one occasion seriously threatened the hotel.

Father wrote in his diary that summer of 1883 that he had had "much conference with Dr. Trudeau regarding arrangements for a sanitarium for the study and cure of tuberculosis."

Dr. Trudeau first suggested the idea to him when sailing home from a boat race, and Father immediately offered to subscribe the first $500 if Dr. Trudeau decided to build one.

Mother took a very great interest too and later had a fair on the island, which will be described in due course. Still later she raised, through her own efforts, an endowment fund of $100,000.

When we were children the little island opposite the Trudeau camp was always known as Bunny Island (although it was called Chicken Island in his deed). We called it Bunny Island because it was here that Dr. Trudeau kept the rabbits of his famous experiment, when he infected a number with T.B. germs and then put half of them out in the fresh air on the little island while the other half were put in his cellar in Saranac. As most of you know, the rabbits on Bunny Island were able to throw off the

13

disease and survive, while those condemned to the cellar all died.

Although Father gave the first subscription towards the sanitarium, I like to remember that it was the guides, headed by Dr. Trudeau's own hunting guide, Fitz Hallock, who actually bought him the "Parson's Meadow" (even though to them it seemed a shame to spoil such a good fox runway!) and gave it to him as a surprise when he had definitely decided he wanted to build and on that spot, for this is such a good example of the friendly relations between guides and campers which added so much to the pleasure of early camp life.

They were certainly versatile men, those early guides; they not only knew the best fishing holes and the best runways for deer, but were good cooks and carpenters. Not only could they build you a cabin, but most of the early furniture was fashioned by their hands. (It was what was known as rustic work and was made up of many small pieces of bark-covered wood. I think there still exists on Birch Island a rustic work table much treasured by my mother which was made by the guides and given her by Dr. Trudeau in appreciation of all the work she did for the sanitarium project.) In rough camp they could entertain you all evening around the campfire with tales of their adventures or beat you at fan-tan, their favorite game.

Phin Bennett is the first guide I remember at all, but Warren Sprague, whom most of you knew at the Slades', must have come soon after, for I remember well the delight I felt when he would pick me up and trundle me around camp in his wheel barrow. He was a fine man and we were all devoted to him, and I know he must have been fond of us, too, for one of his daughters was named after me, and one after one of my sisters.

Warren was 6'6" tall, and P. T. Barnum, who used to come to Paul's for the fishing, once offered to take him and his two brothers into his circus as "The Adirondack Giants," an offer that was indignantly refused. Harold says that Warren always reminded him of Kipling's line: "He trod the ling like a hind in spring and stood like a lance at rest."

Bob Huntington remembers how as a boy he was held spellbound by Sylvester Otis' stories of the Civil War, his favorite one being that if he capsized the boat he would sink like a plummet because he was so full of lead from the rebel guns.

Warren Sprague on the "Carries"

Besides the guides, who lived with the campers in their camps, there was always a group in Paul Smith's boathouse ready to take you on hunting or fishing trips or for a row up the lakes.

Many of the early camps were at first what were known as "day camps." They were used by some of the regular habitués of the hotel, who had guides to row them out to spend the day in

The Guides at Paul's

their chosen spots, cook their dinner, and row them back to the hotel again for the night. Mrs. Paton (Rue Rauch's grandmother), who was at Paul's at least as early as 1878, had one of the earliest of these where the Rauch camp is now, and Mrs. Huntington (Bob's grandmother) had one on the Dartes' point very early, too. She first went to Paul's in 1877 with her two sons, Fred and Robert, who spent two months of that summer hunting here.

As the "day camps" were not owned or leased it is hard to tell exactly when they were first used. Paul Smith was very generous about letting people use the sites year after year — so generous that he even let Mrs. Paton, according to Rue, build a cabin on hers although the land didn't belong to him but to Vilas!

16

Miss Scheftel, who built the first cabin on the Trevors' (the one now used for the blind sale), never seems to have owned or leased any property at all.

Mrs. Durkee told me that there was sometimes an arrangement that, if you didn't use your campsite, you lost it, and that she and Mr. Durkee first came up here to "hold down" the Penfold camp while the Penfolds were abroad.

The deeds to the camps run in the following order:

Father's first deed from Mr. Norton March 27, 1877

Father's second deed from the Mutual Life Association July 14, 1883

Farm, Two Tree Island, Chicken Coop Island, Hog Island and High Island. In 1888 Father bought the rest of the land from the Farm to what is now the Hoes', part of which he sold in about 1902 to Judge Townsend (now Townsend and Goddard). Birch Island was sold to the Spauldings with Chicken Coop (later Twin) Island and Two Tree Island, which has been split in two by the raising of the water level. Their daughter, Alice Paolozzi, lives there now. Hog Island (now Pearl) and High Island went to my brother Harold. The Farm was later divided between the Kings, the Vanderbilts, Carlene Townsend, and the Earles. The Vanderbilts sold their piece to the Pratts, who later turned it over to Francis Trudeau. October 8, 1884

Charles M. Lea, also from the Mutual Life Association. (The Garretts bought this in 1888.) October 8, 1883

James Webb. Bought by Mrs. Dickson in 1891. (Now Dorothy Darte's.) September 25, 1885

Rebecca Polhemus October 8, 1885

William Penfold. Six acres originally—he bought more in 1890. (Later owners were Hume and Doing.) October 9, 1885

Augustus Durkee (Munson) February 9, 1886

Susan Paton (Rauch) February 9, 1886

Serafina Barclay (Blaine)   September 27, 1887
William Richards (Hoe)   September 30, 1887
Dr. Trudeau. Leased July 15, 1886. (John Trevor, Jr.)
                                                       April 15, 1889
Johnstone de Peyster. Leased September 9, 1886. (Huntington)
                                                  September 27, 1886
Bayard Smith. Leased August 2, 1886. (Brewster)
                                                   October 24, 1889
Sarah L. Mitchell (Part now Duncan)   November 5, 1889
H. McK. Twombly (Pratt)   November 19, 1889
Justus Hotchkiss. Leased August 23, 1886. (Patterson)
                                                  December 31, 1889
Henry Hotchkiss. Leased September 11, 1886. (Ely)
                                                  December 31, 1889
Whitelaw Reid. Leased July 15, 1886   April 22, 1890
B. Schlesinger. Leased July 15, 1886. (Hooker-Duncan)
                                                       June 18, 1890
Edward Coates. Leased August 2, 1886. (Earle, Hammond,
   Kent, Garrison)   June 24, 1890
George Cooper. Leased August 5, 1887. This property ran
   from Pulpit Rock north. In 1891 he added what had be-
   longed to S. Barclay.   September 8, 1890
Charles McBurney. Leased in 1886. (Runyon)
                                                  September 8, 1890
Grace Mitchell. Leased March 12, 1887. (Maynard)
                                                  September 8, 1890
Mrs. Alice Huntington (Lawrence)   February 11, 1891
Charles Barney. This was originally part of Dr. Trudeau's
   land. (Trevor)   February 25, 1891
Alvin M. Lothrop (Davies)   November 3, 1897
Graham Lusk (Chace)   September 6, 1902
Anna Lusk (Peterson)   November 22, 1906
J. P. Whiton-Stuart (Mallinson)   May 19, 1922

Besides what remains of old cabins on Birch Island and the Farm and at the Trevors' and the Rauches', there are two little very early cabins in what was the Parish camp next to the Drakes', and I believe one of the cabins in the Smith camp (recently bought by Helen Reid) is very old, too. The guide house at our old Camp Arrowhead,[2] now the Pattersons', was, I was told, the original sitting room moved from where the lake cabin stands, and I believe the Bayard Smith sitting room was moved too and turned into a bedroom when the Brewsters came. I presume there must also be cabins of very early vintage at the Elys', Penfolds' (Humes') and Munsons'.

The camp fire at the Elys' still occupies the identical spot that it did when Mr. and Mrs. Hotchkiss first came to day camp on their point.

Quite a number of campers had leases for ninety-nine years on their sites before they bought them, such leases being recorded, amongst others, for Dr. Trudeau, the Schlesingers, Whitelaw Reid, the Coateses, the Bayard Smiths, Johnstone de Peyster (now the Huntingtons), Justus Hotchkiss (his lease included the use of the marsh to the south as "a pasture and landing"), Henry Hotchkiss, and the Coopers. The Trudeaus, Schlesingers, and Reids all got their first leases on the same day.

Mother describes the "regular daily routine" on Birch Island: "We breakfast at eight, at eleven the children bathe, at six we sup and nine retire. The intermediate time we row or drive (in that case we row to the hotel), read, write, etc."

Father hired a "flat-bottomed sailboat used in carrying lumber" to replace the earlier catamaran, and Mother told me that it upset so often it was a common sight to see Father's head sticking out of the water as he swam for home.

Mother often speaks of the cold that first summer: "July 30, thermometer fifty degrees, had a large fire made in front of spare tent and all huddled there for shelter and warmth." The next day it was forty-nine degrees and Father put up a stove. Dr. Trudeau told them he had "been here twelve summers and never known one as cold as this."

In spite of the cold they went out to explore the lakes and found that seven camps had been put up since their earlier visit. These were, in so far as I can make out, the Leas', Frenches', Trudeaus', Reids', Patons', Penfolds', and Coateses'. As mentioned before, many people camped out in places they didn't own, so I have had to go by references in Mother's diary.

My father and Mr. Reid argued long over who had the first camp. They finally agreed that Father owned the first, but that Mr. Reid had the first permanent cabin. It was built in 1882, and a picture of it with the date is proudly borne on their flag to this day.

In the early days the menfolks spent a good deal of time hunting and fishing. Dr. Trudeau was taken hunting lying on balsam boughs in a guide-boat the very first day he was at Paul's.

He says in his autobiography: "As I lay comfortably on the soft boughs in the stern of the boat, with my rifle in reach across the gunwale, my spirits were high and I forgot all the misery and sickness I had gone through in the past two months." He adds: "If any game laws existed in those days, they didn't apply to the Adirondack wilderness, for it was the custom to shoot game and catch fish at any season, provided they were used as food and not sent out of the woods for sale." He claimed that the Adirondacks were a real hunter's paradise, and Mother's diary certainly bears him out, for she mentions many successful hunts, some of them right on our lake, and also many fishing exploits.

Mr. Justus Hotchkiss was apparently a great fisherman, who made marvelous catches on Lake Clear (then known as Big Clear Pond). He and Jimmy Redwood, his guide, would come home on late September afternoons with the bottom of their

20

boat literally covered with trout often weighing from one-half to two pounds each, and my brother Newton, going off for the day with Graham Lusk and the latter's father, once came home with a hundred trout. My brother Anson tells of a similar catch which he made on Blind Brook on the Osgood. These were mostly small. Anson was prouder of a catch of ten trout weighing ten pounds at our brook at the close of the season (September 15). By "our brook" I mean the one that used to be called "Stokes" or "Farm Brook," the one next to George Townsend's.

Sometimes the fishing trips were of much longer duration. In his recollections Newton writes of going at least half a dozen times from Upper St. Regis or Saranac through to "our rough camp on Grass Pond." Their usual course was from the foot of Saranac Lake across Sweeney Carry to the Raquette River, down the Raquette to Tupper Lake, from Tupper Lake across the carry to Horseshoe Pond, then up Bog River to Mud Lake, a total distance of about seventy-five miles.

"Grass Pond," he writes, "was in those days a wild, secluded spot, very seldom visited by anyone except forest rangers and an occasional sportsman who went there to fish from Mud Lake, a mile to the eastward and one of the most famous hunting grounds for deer. Dr. Loomis had discovered this enchanting spot and had built a small camp consisting only of a log cabin and two bark-covered lean-tos. He usually went there for a fortnight's fishing in the autumn, and I believe for many years we were the only other regular visitors. Near the camp site was a wonderful fishing hole, at the mouth of the inlet, where we usually got all the trout we wanted with very little effort, two and sometimes three at a single cast. These trout averaged between a quarter and a half pound each, and we often got pounders; once I landed one that weighed just over four pounds."

These longer trips were by no means uncommon. Robert Garrett looks back to them with special pleasure, and Louis

Slade often went with my brothers Graham and Anson, who considered them quite the high spots of the season. I don't think sleeping bags had been invented. Anson says they used to carry a nine by nine tent to sleep in and a fly to eat under as well as their other equipment. One or more guides went along and slept under the fly. Our menfolks usually went in September, so as to combine both hunting and fishing with the camping and canoeing, but hardly a week went by that we didn't see boats from Raquette or Blue Mountain Lake and other locations passing Birch Island en route to Paul's.

There were marked differences in the way these boats were shaped, and the boys learned to guess where they came from just by looking at them.

I speak of "canoeing" although canvas canoes, such as we use now, weren't seen on the lakes until my brother-in-law, John Hoyt, sent one down from Maine to my sister Ethel when they were engaged. Before that "guide-boats," often known as Adirondack boats, were usually carried, although there were some Rushton canoes (made of wood) and one or two of birchbark.[3]

My brother Newton had Rushton make him a lovely little canoe called the *Deerslayer*. It weighed only thirty-five pounds and was constantly used for many years. I'm not sure that it isn't on Birch Island still.

On one of his camping trips Newton had a rather terrifying experience. He and a friend who was with him would take turns going out "jacking" at night with a guide. (Jacking was done with a lantern to attract the deer. It is no longer legal but used to be one of the accepted ways to hunt.) On this occasion Newton was the one to be left in their lean-to alone, in the dark, in a pouring rain. The guide had regaled them all through supper with tales of wildcats and bears, and Newton confesses to having felt tense and nervous. Suddenly "something heavy landed on top of the lean-to, something alive, for I could hear it gather itself together and move about. I cocked my rifle and sat waiting with a lantern behind me. The 'thing' jumped from the roof to the ground and for a moment I heard nothing. Then with a loud shriek an enormous beast sprang past the fire and into the lean-to." It turned out to be a goose, more than three and one-half feet high. As though this were not enough excitement for one night, he was later sure that he heard bears crunching berries. When the others came in they wouldn't believe him. He couldn't show them evidence of the goose, but in the morning they found the tracks of two big bears.

Apropos of hunting, I want to quote once more from Newton: "In the early days the more energetic members of the family joined occasionally in hunting deer, which at that time were fairly plentiful in the neighborhood. We would start soon after dawn, sometimes with an experienced hunter, engaged especially for the purpose, and two or three dogs. Our course generally lay across the Seven Carries,[4] where we would drop off, one by one, near 'runways' known to be frequented by deer. Here we would make ourselves inconspicuous and comfortable, sometimes alone and sometimes in twos, and often waited for three or four hours while the huntsman searched for fresh tracks and put out the dogs. It was very exciting, listening to the baying of the hounds as they came nearer and nearer, and occasionally, although not very often even in these early days, a great stag or a fat doe would bound along the runway in plain sight of the watchers, who frequently were so excited that they shot wild. But now and then we had the great satisfaction of returning triumphant to the camp with venison. The waiting hours were not always tiresome, especially for the twosomes, which usually consisted of a young man and maiden and more than once resulted in more permanent associations." He goes on to speak of one summer in particular when there happened to be a large number of young people on the lake, and deer hunting was very popular: "There were very few singles; almost all of the company hunted in pairs."

I think Lord Bryce[5] must have heard exaggerated accounts of these hunting parties, for in the first edition of his *American Commonwealth*, speaking of the freedom from restraint enjoyed by American women, he refers to camping trips in the Adirondacks, telling how a group of young people "engage three or four guides, embark with guns and fishing rods, tents, blankets, and a stock of groceries, and pass in boats up the rivers and across the lakes of this wild country through sixty or seventy miles of trackless forest to their chosen camping ground at the foot of some tall rock that rises from the still crystal of the lake. Here they build their bark hut and spread their beds of the elastic and fragrant hemlock boughs; the youths roam about during the day, tracking the deer, the girls read and work and bake the corn cakes; at night there is a merry gathering round the fire or a row in the soft moonlight. On these expeditions brothers will take their sisters and cousins, who bring perhaps some lady friends with them; the brothers' friends will come too; and all will live together in a fraternal way for weeks or months, though no elderly relative or married lady be of the party." I think Lord Bryce discovered later that this account was, to say the least, a bit exaggerated, for in the later editions of his book this delightful description has been omitted.

Although so much time was spent in hunting and fishing, social life was not neglected. Mother speaks of going with Father to call on Miss Reid and of "dressing" to call on Mrs. Trudeau and Mrs. French, but evidently the "dressing" was not too formal, for she writes later: "I do like the freedom of this place in the way of dress. Even calls are made in flannel suits and gentlemen wear knickerbockers and coarse stockings."

Speaking of dressing, the freedom Mother mentions went

Father and Mother in Calling

right on until I was grown up, and some of us took a firm stand against evening clothes. We always told our guests not to bring them, and I believe Dr. James, after due notice, even went so far as to throw a guest in the lake because he came all dressed up. However, evening dress did finally creep in. I once saw one of our neighbors in full evening dress and bedecked with diamonds paddling in a canoe with a man in a "boiled" shirt en route to a dinner at the Vanderbilts!

It was the Vanderbilts, by the way, who put the Japanese touch to the Pratt camp. When they took it over from the Twomblys they had just returned from a trip to Japan. They thought our lake very Japanese and Whiteface the image of Fujiyama, so they sent for an army of little Japs, who had just completed the Japanese Village for the Buffalo World's Fair, to come and make their camp over. They not only had the cabins Japanized, they dressed all their maids in kimonos! They had taken over a stout English maid of Mother's, and she nearly died of embarrassment when she had to appear before us in this odd new uniform.

The Vanderbilts were not the first to use Japanese trimmings in camps. Mother writes of spending much time "prettying up," and "prettying up," as you can see in the accompanying picture, apparently consisted of hanging up as many Japanese fans and

"Prettied Up"

ornaments as space would permit. I think all of the earliest camps went in for some such Japanizing.

Father was Commodore of the Yacht Club from its inception (I have written little of that important institution because Harold has covered the ground so fully in the Fiftieth Anniversay Yacht Club Book),[6] and every year he gave a yacht club dinner to the men who belonged. The time came when he felt that in politeness to his guests, who most of them dressed in the evenings, he should wear a dinner coat too. We protested but Father was firm and sent for his coat to Lenox. When the night of the party arrived Father sat at the head of the table in all his glory, but there wasn't another tuxedo to be seen. All the guests, in deference to what they knew was Father's preference in camp, had come in camp clothes.

It was soon after this that our nice green yacht club coats were introduced so that everyone would know "what the well-dressed man should wear."

Mother also mentions people paying dinner calls. This in connection with their first dinner party attended by Dr. and Mrs. Trudeau, Dr. Waldon, Miss Reid, Walter Phelps (afterwards ambassador to Germany), and Dr. and Mrs. French. The tables were decorated with "a beautiful collection of toadstools, all colors, arranged tastefully in pie plates, and surrounded with wreaths of lilies from the river."

Dinners were not the only form of entertainment. Miss Penfold had a "Four O'clock Welsh Rabbit, about seventy-five there and very enjoyable"; and Mrs. Paton had a "Welsh Rabbit" too.

People evidently stayed up later in the season in the early days. The Penfold Welsh Rabbit party took place on September 26, and Mother speaks of a full church on September 16 and of two hundred and fifty people at the hotel September 20. She also remarks that the visitors at the hotel are much more "select," the habitués having taken the place of the earlier transients.

Our First Dining Room

Mother missed the Penfold party because she had to stay home to talk to "Baker" about the building of a cabin. They agreed on "three ordinary log huts joined together with shingle roofs and painted ends" which were to cost $775. They had planned more elaborate buildings but found the estimates too high, three or four builders wanting $2,500. They decided that simpler cabins would be "quite as well for our use."

They certainly proved themselves so, for there they stood, with only the addition of a bay window or two, until I was quite grown up, and even now when you go into Alice Paolozzi's dining room you pass through what is left of one of these original cabins. Father said that the brick chimney cost as much as all the rest of the building, as the bricks had to be transported so far.

Baker was a French Canadian named Joseph Boulanger, who translated his name because so many people had trouble with it. He owned Baker's Carry,[7] where our landing now is.

On September 29 the family broke camp. It had been such a pleasant summer that everyone hated to leave, but with the temperature at twenty-nine degrees, eating out-of-doors no longer seemed "just the thing to enjoy." Even then they found it hard to leave the woods entirely; they stayed on at Paul's until that closed in October, and then with some of the other guests moved over to Miller's on Saranac Lake.

In June of 1884 the family returned to camp. This time they hired a coach and six horses and had a "delightful ride." It took them only six hours, including stopping for mails, for they changed horses three times.

Later this long drive was much shortened, for Paul Smith's station was built at what is now Gabriels. Dorothy Darte remembers this approach particularly and the thrill that it gave her to drive in the coach from there to the hotel, eat a marvelous breakfast, and then row up to camp, eight in one row boat besides hand bags! Paul Smith's became Gabriels at a much later date when the line was run in from Lake Clear to the hotel, and two "Paul Smith's" seemed unnecessary.

Father couldn't come until later, so Mother wrote him that "the house is just as nice, even nicer than I expected." She was also much pleased with the "small two-story house with open fireplace" which Newton, who had come to camp early, had built at a cost of $100, and with the "very substantial and pretty breakwater and lighthouse" which he always spoke of as his first architectural creation.

The "two-story house," turned around and with bay windows and dressing room added and the ceiling taken out so that now it has only one story, still stands on Birch Island, probably the second oldest building on the lake. It used to face the water but was unfortunately turned around when a guest tent was put between it and the view.

They had fifteen tents in camp besides the cabins: five fourteen by fourteen; six nine by nine; three seven by seven; and the original dining tent.

Our First "Main Cabin"
(from the left: Ethel, Mildred, and Carrie)

The breakwater you must all remember, although it was so often renewed through the years that it couldn't have had a single original board left in it when Mrs. Spaulding took it down. The light which hung in the "lighthouse" at the end was supposed to show belated travelers the way from Baker's Carry to Paul Smith's.

Mother found a well dug, too, with "delicious water clear as from Able Spring"—a great improvement, for the year before they had to row all the way to the spring opposite what is now the Duncans' camp for water.

Mother wasn't so pleased with what had happened at the farm as she was with the work in camp. There a strip of trees, which was to have been left all along the water front, had been burned down. "Makes one's heart sick to see it," wrote Mother. "It will never amount to anything."

Mother was also disturbed because the case of claret left in Baker's keeping had disappeared, as well as the things in the ice house. "Another year," she writes, "we had better hire a room at Paul's as others do unless we can better protect the ice house." She also writes of the "amusing competition" between Plato and Miller, who were both so anxious to get our freight that they offered to carry it for forty-five cents a hundred. I presume all the way from Plattsburg.

The Breakwater

31

The breakwater, besides being "substantial and pretty," was a great delight to us children. Within its sheltered harbor we learned to swim and row in safety. (Little red life preservers were not yet the fashion.) We sailed our boats here too, and fished, and it made it easy for our nurses to pull us out when, as so often happened, we fell in. The elders used to sit on this dock in the evenings and think that from there the camp, with all its lanterns alight, looked like fairyland.

Nothing is said about chickens that second summer, but Mother tells of an early trip to McCarthy's to buy sheep, as both the cook and Warren were quite willing to butcher and dress them and they could be kept "on the old cow island." She ordered a buckboard from the hotel for the trip and was surprised when "Mr. Paul Smith himself" turned up to take her with his fine new team—"very pleasant, for it saved so much time."

She bought thirty-six sheep, at three dollars each, to be delivered eight at a time, "a great saving as the butcher asked ten dollars," and was satisfied that with these sheep and the potatoes, which Newton had arranged for her to buy at twenty-five cents a bushel, housekeeping was going to be much easier.

Another housekeeping help was the telephone, which, believe it or not, was installed on Birch Island that same summer. On it they could talk to Paul Smith's, Saranac, and Bloomingdale, the latter being at that time the shopping center; but Mother complains that with it camp "doesn't feel so campy," the first sign of that conservatism in everything to do with camp and camp life for which we "old-timers" have always been noted. Newton, Phelps Smith, and Joe Baker put up the line and even, I believe, got a franchise for it. Newton also, that summer, marked out the first road from the farm to Paul Smith's. The trees were cut and the road made the following winter. Part of the road went just where it does now, but in two places, one in Penfold Bay (or East Bay as it was called) and one in the lower lake, we drove along beaches. These beaches, together with the one in front of the Rauch camp, were once quite extensive, but the last traces of them were obliterated when the dam, which raised the lakes more than a foot, was built on the river.

Driving on Penfold Bay Beach

Raising the water also wiped out two islands: the little one between the Trevors' and the Pratts', which used to be quite big enough to land on, and Little Island, mentioned in the Huntingtons' deed, next to Gull Rock on Spitfire.

Sunday night hymn sings seem to have started July 27, 1884. At least that is the date on which Mother first wrote, "In the evening we had singing." Quite a record to have kept up for sixty-nine years.

By August plans for building Dr. Trudeau's sanitarium were well under way. Mother volunteered to hold a fair at Birch Island to raise money, and many ladies offered to make articles.

By September 2 the work and fancy articles were all sent up, and "we had a fine display." A lot of things were made right on Birch Island, where the twenty-seven occupants all worked hard. "Even the servants worked," wrote Mother, "turning to in the evenings when their regular work was done, for all were much interested."

Mother had a wonderful imagination. She had a grab bag made which was the best I have ever seen. A pillow and a stuffed mask were fastened to the top of a barrel. A sun bonnet covered the head, and a calico dress with ample folds covered the rest. The large pocket in the skirt came right over a good-sized hole that had been made in the barrel, so we children could put our hands right into Aunt Jemima's pocket and pull out a surprise. What fun it was!

More money came in after the fair, including forty dollars for photographs taken by Mr. Durkee, so that before the season was over they had eleven hundred dollars.

This sanitarium fair became an annual event, first at Birch Island and then at Paul's, and people vied with each other in planning salable articles. Our greatest success was with the little tent sewing baskets that Mother invented. She had us cover cardboard with green and white striped material and sew the pieces together to form miniature tents. You lifted one side of the top and there, inside, were needles and threads, silks, scissors, thimble, etc. They went like hot cakes, and we had many orders for more.

In later years on our biennial trips abroad, Mother spent much time collecting unusual things of charm and value which she knew could be sold at a profit at the fair, and quite a bit of money was raised in this way.

We had a bad fire in camp that September, and although I was not yet four I can still remember the roaring sound that it made. Mother had had a fire in her tent, and in some way the tin shield

Mother, Ethel, and Carrie on the platform of the tent which burned. Note Newton's cabin still facing the lake.

of the stovepipe must have slipped. Luckily Father was away, and she was sleeping in my sister's tent, for everything except Mother's "best dinner dress" was consumed in less than five minutes, and had she been there, I don't see how she could have escaped without serious injury.

Before leaving camp that fall, Mother wrote Father that she had arranged with Phin to "build stable on mainland, shingle the storeroom behind my tent, build a summer house and rustic seats, clear up the path around the island, put double floors in the tents and paint boats, clean tents, etc."; but she wonders if she had not better arrange with Noakes, "who has oxen and everything," to do it at once as it seems quite a lot of work.

Apropos of the storeroom behind her tent, this is perhaps as good a place as any to explain how our camps took on their unusual form and grew up into little villages instead of developing into houses. At first we all lived in tents, as you know, so they were naturally separate. Tents couldn't be left up over the winter, and Mother found it very inconvenient to move all the furniture into the cabin and back and hit upon the scheme of building little wooden storerooms behind the tents into which the furniture could be moved. When the tents wore out it was a natural transition to add to these storerooms by putting cabins instead of tents in front. Often the old tent floors were used. This transition shows very plainly in the two tent cabins on Birch Island and the row at the Earles'. Guide houses, carpenter shops, and ice houses all fitted well into this unit system, and pretty soon it became the accepted way to build, even if you had never had any tents.

There were a number of outstanding events to mark the summer of 1885. In the first place there was a "tornado" which Mother describes as "terrific." Six men worked through all the storm hanging on to flies and tents and tightening ropes, but in spite of their efforts one tent was badly torn and partly blown down. Four trees on the island fell and one was struck by lightning.

Then the President, Grover Cleveland, came for a visit at Paul's, and Father, Mother, and I presume many others rowed down and met him. Then there was the second Sanitarium Fair, this time accompanied by a very successful play, *Garrick Fever*, and guideboat races; and there was a visit of inspection to the sanitarium itself, where "everything is very nice and so tasty. So many things have been given towards furnishing that it is much more sumptuous than it otherwise would have been." It was already full, and Dr. Trudeau was having tents put up.

Louis Slade came up for his annual visit, and Mother wrote Father that she was having the boys build a laundry, not because she really needed one but because it was hard enough to keep "Newton and Graham and Anson out of trouble anyway. With Louis in camp too it would be impossible unless they had something to keep them busy."

Mother had a bedroom cabin built too, that summer, to replace the burned tent, and a new boat house with a covered deck on top; and the old boat house tent was moved a little to the north to be a guest room.

The Sanitarium Fair

Boat houses were a great problem before we learned to put them on really solid foundations. This boat house had to be replaced by a log one some time in the nineties, and still later by the present one. A little guest cabin which replaced the guest tent on the water proved difficult to look after too, so it was pulled across the ice to the farm, where it still is.

The Birch Island Landing

We had three successive living rooms after the "parlor" tent, but that was because we outgrew the old ones. First the little log cabin built in 1884 was added to in the nineties by the addition of a new log room. Then the present main cabin was built in about 1905, incorporating the old dining room as a writing room but destroying the rest of the original building. I made good use of the new writing room, for that was the year Ransom and I became engaged.

Mother's cabin had a thatched roof at first, but that didn't prove practical, so the thatch was later replaced by shingles.

In September, 1885, Mother writes that she has just been to see the Reids' new cabin: "Very pretty, just suited for a young lady." (Whitelaw Reid's niece lived on their point before he did. Like so many others, she seems to have built before they owned.)

Last but not least, 1885 was the year of the first yacht "club." The members were Dr. Trudeau, my father, my brother Newton, and Mr. Lea. Mother offered a cup, still used as a sugar bowl on Pearl Island, and the first race was set for July 23rd. Alas, as you can see in the picture there was no wind. So it had to be sailed over later.

The First Boat Rac

The "Sail Off"

That first cup was closely related to the trickman's "now you see it and now you don't," for although Father won it with that first race he had to turn it over the very next day to Dr. Trudeau, who in turn had to hand it over to Mr. Lea before the week was up. The winner of the most races took it home for the winter, but it was raced for again the next year and some years after, for you had to win the most races for three years to keep it.

In 1883, 1884, and 1885 my own memories are few and far between: Warren and his wheelbarrow, the grab bag at the fair, the fire at night, sleeping in the tent, and Mother photographing my sisters and me as we leaned out of the cabin window—that is about all. (Mother, by the way, was an ardent photographer before the days of snap shots. She had a flat-bottomed boat made to carry her and her camera safely, and I can still picture her drifting about the lake with the camera on its tripod before her and a shawl over it and her head, so that she could see the image in the ground glass plate. Most of the pictures I have reproduced are hers.) After that, my own memories come thick and fast, memories of childhood days, of the old coach, of buckboard drives over corduroy roads, of fishing from the breakwater, and our disappointment when Mother ruled that no cook could be asked to skin and cook a catfish, of happy swimming times, all too short for us, because Dr. Trudeau, who looked after us, thought it was bad to stay more than twenty minutes in fresh water and Mother or a nurse always hovered nearby, watch in hand; of the comfort of our dear Anna Valet's hand reaching for mine in a thunderstorm at night; of Fanny, our little fawn, and of playing house in the tangled roots of the one big pine which gave the name of "Pine Tree Side" to the south side of Birch Island. The thrill of leading people "around the island" for the first time—and most thrilling of all, the day when Mr. Drake didn't come to start the boat race, and I, at the age of six or so, was allowed to officiate, Father's watch tightly clutched in one hand and a handkerchief held high in the other to be dropped at the ordained moment.

Memories of girlhood days and adolescence—"puppy" love and jolly house parties—and of the happy summer when Ransom and I decided to "play house" together for the rest of our lives—and later memories of those early years on Spitfire, where, in our own camp, surrounded by good friends and with our children growing up happily in the old camp traditions, we spent what were perhaps the happiest summers of all.

Pine Tree Side was not the only part of Birch Island to have a special name. There was Horseshoe Bay, Birdie Hollow, Crystal Hollow, and Blueberry Hill, and the northwest end of the island was always known as the Guide's Camp. When Father had our little log playhouse built as a surprise, it was Goldilocks Hall, and when he first led us to it there was a bear looking out of the window. That same bear is old now, and tame, and Alice has taught him to stand in her living cabin and hold umbrellas.

Fanny was found swimming all alone in the lake and brought in to be a pet for Carrie and me. We kept her in a stockade between Newton's cabin and the lake.

A Visit with Fanny

When the autumn came and we were leaving, Father had Warren take her over to the farm and build a pen for her there with orders to keep food always in the pen. Once she was at home there the gate was to be left open, so that she could come or go as she wished. We made her a red collar, hoping that hunters would see that she was a pet. Fanny and Warren's deer hound became great friends, and once when she was chased into camp by other hounds, he fought them off and let her get away.

There is another animal story I like to remember. A man came to Paul's with a performing bear, and the bear got loose and strayed away. His owner was distressed, not only at losing the bear, but because he feared she would starve to death, as she had never learned to hunt for food — it just came as a reward for doing her tricks. All the men in the neighborhood were begged to join in a hunt, and this they did, spreading out through the woods so that they covered a considerable territory. Suddenly, one man halted, almost unable to believe his eyes. There, in a clearing, was that hungry little bear trustfully going through her tricks so that food would be provided!

Burgess would never be at a loss for material for his animal stories if he lived up here with us. Ever since I can remember there have been two shelldrake families, a big one and a little one (I have always wondered if they have a law of primogeniture, for how else can they decide which of the fifteen or twenty babies is to come back). Then there have always been two loons on St. Regis Pond and, more recently, on ours; red-winged blackbirds and "long legs" on the lower slough; beavers building their wonderful houses; foxes, rabbits, coons and porcupines in abundance; and the great white-headed American eagle, soaring above us, turning his head from side to side as though loathe to miss any of our interesting doings; and the frogs! how we listened for and welcomed their croaking chorus when we came home to Birch Island.

One year camp had been rented to a family who looked upon frogs not as old friends but as table delicacies. Hardly a croak bade us welcome home; everyone was upset. My sister Carrie and I decided something must be done about it and set out for

Chickadee Creek armed with red flannel, string, and fish nets. Not for us the bows and arrows which the Conservation Department now claims you need a license for. We just tied a piece of the flannel to a string and threw it out near a frog, who would seize it in his teeth and hang on for dear life, making it simple to slide a net under him and haul him out. We went home with a boat load. Unfortunately we didn't just turn them loose in our own deserted frog haunts. We had what seemed to us the brilliant idea of having Mr. Hochard, the chef, bake a crust and put it over a big dishpan with all the frogs inside, and Barton, the butler, was told to pass it to Mother. Mother, thanks to our big family and countless guests, wasn't a bit daunted by the enormous size of the dish presented to her. She just opened it up with the spoon, and out hopped the frogs. She was quite cross with us, almost the only time that I ever knew her to be so. We said it wasn't fair, for only a short time before she had had the butler bring in a live pig on a platter and thought it funny, though the pig had jumped down from the platter, and the great Dane had run after the pig, and we had all had to run after the great Dane; quite a boar hunt that didn't end until we caught the great Dane and rescued the pig out near Goldilocks Hall.

Speaking of renting camp, there was a time in the gay nineties when our lakes were very fashionable and camps in much demand. So few were ever available to renters that they brought fantastic prices, probably the highest summer rentals in America. It was, if I remember aright, the Clarence Mackays who ate our frogs; but they paid $12,000 for the privilege of doing so for some six weeks. I believe the rent included ice and wood and the services of a guide, but at that time no camps had either plumbing or electricity.

No tale of local fauna would be complete without mention of the beguiling little ball of white fluff who grew up under the Chace's loving care to become "Careless Love." Careless was a seagull who learned to take food from your hand and answer to her name, even coming down out of the skies when you called her, to sit on the gunwale of your boat and open her mouth for food. She spent the summer on our lake and then flew away just as she was to be banded, and so far as anyone knows never came back, though for a year or two cries of "Careless, Careless" greeted all the gulls that appeared.

For the benefit of the very young who may not remember them, I cannot forbear to mention our chipmunks and Hammy King's, even though they don't belong to early days. Ours were wartime pets who would come running when we called them, and would bring their friends, and all eat from our hands; one of them, Ringtail, followed us around like a little dog. We fed them for years. The year we moved into Camp Red Pines I went back to the old camp and called them, but to my disappointment got no response. Two years later I was walking in the woods with Ransom some distance from where our chipmunk friends used to be. I called his attention to a chipmunk who somehow looked familiar, but I think he thought me crazy. I didn't call, for I had no food to offer, but we returned a day or two later to the same spot well provided with nuts and crackers. I must have called nearly five minutes. Nothing happened, and I thought probably I was crazy and turned to go home. Just as I turned I caught sight of a flying bit of fur, and there, running for all he was worth from far in the woods, came a chipmunk who, after sniffing carefully around me, climbed on my knee to be fed. Pretty good, I think, to remember my voice for over two years.

Hamilton King's chipmunk not only came to be fed but learned to do tricks like walking a tight rope and jumping through a ring. He was known as Willy until he disappeared for weeks and then came back, as Hammy described it, "wearing a double-breasted waistcoat with two rows of buttons." After that, "he" became Wilhelmina.

Sailing was an interest that grew in importance as I grew older. When I was a child, women didn't sail. They congregated on the observation roof of our boathouse and drank tea and gossiped while watching the races, which always started and finished between the islands opposite camp to give them a good view. Mother, who always held advanced views, wrote to Father when I was only six, that she didn't see why the girls shouldn't enjoy sailing too, "though of course not in the big boats." And when I was about fourteen we all did take to it, and not so long after that Elsie Ely and Jean Reid and I were all sailing Idems.[8] I got the chance only in stormy weather when Father couldn't sail on account of his sciatica.

Until I was about fifteen my sister Carrie and I seldom left the island except to go on excursions up the mountain, or over the carries, or perhaps to the Wawbeek on Saranac Lake or over the Sangemo Trail.

To climb the mountain, in earliest days, you started way over towards Paul Smith's and took a long trail past a hermit's camp, but that was before I was old enough to go. We always rowed to the end of the lake, carried over into Spectacle, rowed across that, and walked up from there. The present trail was made by CCC boys, who had a camp not far from Paul Smith's during the depression. Our old trail was made almost impassable by the terrible fire which burned all our side of the mountain when I was about sixteen.

The Sangemo Trail was, I believe, the first trail between "Big Clear Pond" and our lake. It went in back of our present landing towards Chickadee Creek and came out near what is now the hotel on Lake Clear. An old Indian lived there and used, so Robert Garrett says, to keep a horse and a little wagon and transport boats from one lake to the other. I can't remember the Indian and his one-horse cart, but I remember well the two-horse wagons able to carry about four boats at a time which used to

Boat Wagon on Baker's Carry

bring our boats home after our trips over the carries.

When we went over the carries, we didn't just go to St. Regis Pond and back. From St. Regis Pond we carried to Little Clear, then to Upper Saranac for lunch at the Inn (then known as the Prospect House). After lunch we paddled down a long stream to Big Clear, and then walked home over Baker's Carry or the Sangemo Trail.

There was always such a campful of us that we weren't interested in outside playmates and quite resented it when we were made to go and play with the little girls who came every summer to visit the Hotchkisses and the Durkees, but after I was fifteen the picture changed.

House parties had always been a feature of Birch Island life, and a stream of English people and foreigners kept turning up with letters of introduction. (Once one of Queen Victoria's granddaughters asked to come, but fortunately for our peace of mind she changed her plans.) Now we younger ones began to have house parties of our own. What plans we made for them! The invitations were sent out months ahead, after much consultation, for not only must the guests be congenial as a group, but some, especially amongst the men, must be more congenial to one daughter and some to the others; and there was always great excitement after our guests arrived as to who would invite whom to go rowing after supper.

We had supper early so as not to interfere with the sunset, and then hurried down in couples to the boathouse. The men would row or paddle us while we sat in the stern facing them, ensconced in cushions.

When I was fifteen, Anson persuaded Mother that I was staying out too late with my best beau, so Mother ruled that *everyone* was to come in by ten o'clock, and she used to stand on the breakwater and ring the dinner bell for us as a signal to start for home. When we got in we all repaired to the dining room, where we regaled ourselves with milk and gingerbread bunloaf and talk before going to bed. I soon learned to spend my evenings in the bay towards Keese Mills. It took longest to come home from there.

I got to know the bay very well, not only because of its advantages as an evening resort but because Louis Slade and Mabel and Ruth Hoe and I used to pull up our boats there every Sunday afternoon and walk over the trail to Keese Mills to teach Sunday school to the guides' children in the Presbyterian church.

Mr. Lusk, the "Rev" whom we all know, had just been called there and needed help. I believe it was Mrs. Paton's suggestion that there should be a church at Keese Mills, for at that time the people in the village knew little of the outside world and not much about Christianity. I remember one of my little girls bursting into tears when I told the story of the crucifixion and saying it was the saddest story she had ever heard. The "Rev," as they all came to call him, did a wonderful work there. He was

48

always ready to get up at any hour of the night to go on snow-shoes to a sick neighbor or to do anything else he could to help.

The first square dance I ever went to was a benefit gotten up by the guides to help build him a rectory. It was winter, and I was in camp with the Slades. We drove down over the frozen lakes in a sleigh and then up the river, a most beautiful drive, and I can remember the caller singing out, "Birdy in the center and Hawky outside." We may have been far from civilization, but for supper they gave us raw oysters! (Out of a can.)

The house parties on Birch Island were not the only ones. The Reids always had a camp full of people, young and old, and other campers had guests too, so we young folks began to do much more visiting from camp to camp.

My Sister Helen Has a House Party

49

If like Mother in earlier days I tried to list a typical day's activities at that time, it would go something like this: breakfast, 8:30 to 9:30; tennis most of the morning; swimming before lunch; sailing in the afternoon; tea at 4:30 or 5:00; supper at 6:30; canoeing until 10:00; refreshments and talk in the dining room until about 11:00; then bed.

The girls all lived in the front part of our camp; the men in "bachelors' row" facing Pearl Island.

At least once a week we went up the mountain and over the carries, feeling that each new batch of guests must be taken on at least these two excursions. Riding was sandwiched in too, for Father always kept horses at the farm.

I think the most strenuous day of my life was one when after tennis all morning and racing a boat in the afternoon, I hurried over to the farm to ride with a friend who was visiting at Paul's, then went to supper at Mrs. Blaine's (she had rented the Mitchell camp), where we ate at a trestle table under the trees and the guides cooked our supper on an open fire; but the butler poured champagne into our tin cups and passed around creme de menthe afterwards! Then I carried a boat over the Keese Mills Trail to the river, and we rowed home up the river and through the lakes.

Both the Reids and ourselves kept a sort of open house on our tennis courts. All who wanted to play came without invitation armed with racquets. It was not customary to stop in the middle of the set, but as soon as one was completed we tossed up to see who would play next. One set once went to 28-26, which I think must have been an all-time record.

Mrs. Reid once told me, as I sat with her in the summer house overlooking the tennis, that she had been to many courts during her years abroad but "never found a court that I enjoyed as I do this one." She added that she loved camp more than any other place. She liked to share this pleasure, and the camp was

50

kept filled with interesting people of all kinds.

Mrs. Reid was a great democrat in the broadest sense of the word, and protocol played a very minor part in life at Camp Wildair. I remember once after I was married, Ransom and I were lunching there with our children when, glancing around the table, I saw that Mrs. Reid had put a young missionary, with whom she wished to talk, on her right, while our young Milly, aged about fourteen, sat between a bishop and an ambassador, and Whitey Reid's governess on the ambassador's other side.

Mr. Reid was, of course, an important man who held a number of important posts, but I will always remember him as the kind host who was the first to talk to me as one grown-up to another.

The first tennis tournament I remember was the summer that I was sixteen when Ogden Reid and I managed to get into the semi-finals. The last was in the summer of 1940 when Pete and I won the consolation prize at the combined age of one hundred

The Ark *at Baker's Carry (Hoe Point in background)*

51

and twenty-eight. Through all the years tennis has been a great source of pleasure to me, especially when Ransom and I could play together. Even now that I am over seventy and my hand has lost its cunning, I still enjoy a sort of make-believe game with my children and grandchildren.

One of the things that made it easier to get around and be sociable was the coming of launches. When we had only rowboats and slides or "slips" to land them at instead of docks, dining and visiting were pretty well confined to fair weather. If you sat in the stern of a rowboat in the rain and then ran the boat up a slide, all the water in the bottom of the boat ran up your legs and over your knees, and no amount of umbrellas or waterproofs did you any good. It wasn't until launches came in that we all built docks. Even Father's old sailboat, the *Delos*, a cat in which he raced for years, was built with a bottom that sloped towards the bow so that it could run up a slide, too. As a result, it had a frisky way of kicking up its heels and going over bow first, which was rather disconcerting.

I think the first launch was what Robert Garrett calls "a horrible naphtha launch which came up the Hudson by its own power and then was brought to camp somehow, by train or wagon or both." The Earles had a very early one, too, and there were some at Paul's, but they proved noisy and dangerous, several of them actually burning up, so they were soon discarded. They were with us long enough, however, to ruin a nice custom. Hymn Sing had moved from our main cabin to the lake, where we would congregate in rowboats and canoes with Louis Slade and Sam Evans (Ellen Hoe's husband) singing a little extra loud to carry us along. When Paul Smith's acquired naphtha launches the visitors there began to treat us as a sort of show and would circle round and round us without ever joining in. It wasn't very pleasant, so we went back to singing indoors.

We didn't always sing on Birch Island. Sometimes we sang

52

at the Hoes', and one summer we sang at the Garretts' and another we moved from one camp to another until finally we settled down at the Slades' to continue there until we took over after Louis' death.

After the naphtha launches there were some big electric ones big enough to hold a whole family, but they had to go down to Paul's to be charged, so they weren't very practical.

Francis Trudeau says that his *Little Devil* was the first speedboat on the lakes. When he was interning at Bellevue Hospital in 1913-14, Dr. Trudeau, remarking that his electric boat was a little slow, asked to be allowed to use the fast one. He came to our camp in it one day, and when I told him that I was shocked to see an old-timer like him using one of the horrible noisy things, he replied that if I had to sit still watching everybody else go by I would enjoy as he did being able to go faster than any of them. Francis has written me about this: "Naturally, I was delighted to have him do it. Of course in those days there were no self-starters, so during the good days in the summer he had a man come over from the Hotel, start the boat around 10 A.M. and then leave it run until he wanted to go out, at which time he would sail up the lake at full speed and thoroughly enjoy beating everyone in sight. When he wished to call on anyone he would land at the dock and, unless there was a guide available to start the boat for him again after the call, he would simply leave it running. He would often spend a whole morning this way and never turn the engine off until he got back to the Hotel."

By the time that Ransom and I had our own first camp on Spitfire, there was a great deal of community activity. Sailboat racing, which had gone into temporary eclipse during the first World War, had been revived (largely through the efforts of our young Ransom, who had rowed around to all the yacht owners and asked them to join in a race). For Ransom and me these revived races were a great interest. The children each had an "O" boat, and when race days came around there was great competition between Ransom and Milly in the *Owl* and Son and me in the *Clytie*.

Besides the racing there was lots of tennis always going on on the new entoutcas courts and golf at the St. Regis River Golf Club, and dinners and lean-to parties (at which Kitty Chace would sing delightfully even after innumerable pancakes), and charade parties, not to mention the annual tournaments and the fancy dress dance at the Reids' in the Labor Day week end.

A feature of these parties was that they were not segregated as to ages. Except for dinners everyone over fifteen played around together. A group of young people once came to me and asked if I couldn't "do something" about a party to which no elders had been invited. They felt that camp customs were in jeopardy.

We had a wonderful party for Mother's eightieth birthday. Seven of her nine children were able to be there with all their families. There was a huge birthday cake adorned with eighty little pine trees donated by the forestry people, and a "Jack Horner pie" in the big china frog that we still use as a scrap basket. After supper Mother laughed until she cried at the tableaux we staged, all of us posing as we had in childhood pictures. Anson, with his beard, taking milk from a bottle was the most ridiculous of all. This, by the way, was a strictly family party.

And speaking of family parties, I must mention that very important one for us, Milly and Dyson's wedding. This, though a family party in one way, was also a community party, for everyone turned to and helped in a most wonderful way, from the sending out of the invitations to the wedding breakfast itself, where our neighbors' boys acted as waiters and practically every camp kitchen supplied something towards the menu. To add to the excitement, Ransom, forgetting that for once he didn't have

54

on rubber soles, slipped on the deck of the Earles' launch, waxed and polished for the occasion, and fell into the lake, almost but not quite causing a delay in the proceedings.

The church looked lovely decorated with whole birch trees, evergreens, and ferns, Milly carried a big bunch of waterlilies, and the bridesmaids carried pine branches, and after the service it took a whole flotilla of launches to ferry the two hundred guests to camp.

One of the best parties of all was the one which celebrated Louis Slade's Golden Jubilee. Caroline and Louis had made themselves a very important place, not only in the community but in the hearts of their neighbors, and when Louis was heard to remark that he hadn't missed coming to the woods a single summer in fifty years, we all thought something should be done to celebrate. Everybody worked with a will. Caroline was taken into the secret and agreed to accept an invitation from the Spauldings for supper and bridge on the night appointed (we wanted the party to be on Birch Island as that was where Louis had come as a little boy). When they arrived, Louis was amazed to find the Junior Yacht Club drawn up on the dock to greet him with a salute from the Yacht Club cannon. Then he was led to the main cabin where I, dressed as nearly as possible as I had been at three years old (that being my age when he first arrived), recited some verses of welcome, saying that not only those present but still earlier friends wanted to greet him, and then Johnson Garrett walked in dressed and made up to look like my father and bade him welcome, and Ned Trudeau followed, in his grandfather's hunting clothes and carrying the old doctor's gun. Other old-timers appeared too: Ted Pommeroy as Paul Smith, Ransom in a white beard as Mr. Drake, Elsie Ely as Mr. Hotchkiss, Helen Anderson as one of the Penfolds, etc. I wish I had a picture of them all. We all sat down to a supper to which nearly everyone had contributed food; and after supper we had charades, planned well ahead of time, as our charades always were, so as to be really good.

Louis used to complain, when bridge first came in, that we sat up too late—"long past camp bedtime," as he used to put it. So, as a grand finale, we had collected all the alarm clocks on the lake—there must have been over twenty of them—and hidden them under chairs, behind curtains, etc. At nine o'clock they started going off, first one, then another, and when at last they were all quiet we announced that it was Louis' bedtime and

Yacht Club Group, about 1903
left to right, standing: Ogden Reid, L. Bayard Smith, Edward Penfold, Henry Pendleton ...s, Lewis S. Thompson, Jack C. R. Peabody; extreme right: Henry L. Hotchkiss; Whitelaw Reid, Anson Phelps Stokes, Simeon J. Drake, William Hall Penfold)

all must go home. It was the only part of the party that he didn't enjoy.

With Louis' party I think this chronicle should close. In what has happened since you have all had a share and so need no recollections of mine.

If I have written only of the surface things, of customs and characters, sayings and doings, and said nothing of what this place has given through all these years of beauty, peace and inspiration, it is because in these deeper things, too, you have shared; and besides no pen of mine could do them justice.

As a child when anything went wrong, I would say to myself, "Never mind, we're going to the Adirondacks," and just the thought of this place would make me happy again.

I know that according to most authorities the word "Ad-i-ron-dacks" means "tree-eaters" and was used by the Mohawks as a term of derision suggesting that our predecessors were poor hunters. I prefer the definition once seen by Robert Garrett claiming that the word was better translated as "sissy" and that the appellation was given to the Iroquois in this neighborhood because, once they had taken to themselves the peace and beauty of our mountains, woods and waters, they desired nothing better than to settle down here and live at peace themselves.

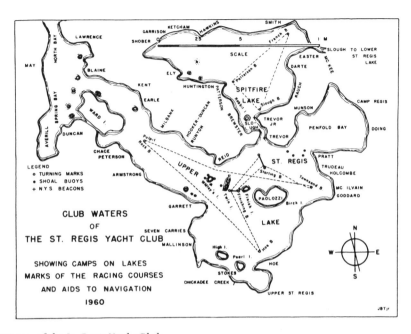

Club Waters of the St. Regis Yacht Club

N O T E S

1. Dr. Alfred L. Loomis, frequent visitor at Paul Smith's, New York physician, and recognized authority on lung diseases during his lifetime (d. 1895).
2. On Spitfire Lake.
3. J. Henry Rushton (1843-1906), designer and builder of boats, turned out cedar canoes and canvas-covered Indian Girl canoes in his shop in Canton, New York. His lightweight cedar canoes, designed for ease in carrying over portages, became celebrated in the 1880's after George W. Sears (pen name "Nessmuk") had used them for three years on Adirondack cruises and praised them in three series of letters in *Forest and Stream.*
4. A series of ponds and carries extending from the Saranac Inn to Paul Smith's (see "Adirondack Canoe Routes," recreational circular of the New York State Conservation Department).
5. British authority on American government and ambassador to Washington 1907-1913, James Bryce made his first visit to the United States in 1870 at thirty-two. Taking home with him enthusiastic impressions and "a swarm of bold generalizations," he worked some of these up into articles on American life. In one of the articles he illustrates his views on the freedom in the relations between the sexes in America by describing unchaperoned mixed hunting parties in the Adirondacks ("On Some Peculiarities of Society in America," *Cornhill Magazine,* December, 1872, p. 707). The young Bryce must have been charmed by the Daisy Millers of the land and missed them on his return home. "England," he writes, "may yet see the day when, instead

of being driven to suggest half furtive meetings at the Academy or the Horticultural, a young gentleman will ask a lady to come for a walk in Kensington Gardens tomorrow from half-past five till seven. Meanwhile, until that happy day arrives, it is pleasant to remember that beyond the Atlantic there is a land where youths and maidens have 'a lovely time,' where . . . friendship is honoured along with love, where friendship leads up to love, and love is all the truer and more lasting because friendship has gone before."

On later trips to the United States Bryce "dropped into the Atlantic" the greater part of his earlier generalizations, but his impressions on the freedom from restraint enjoyed by American girls and women remained intact. In his chapter "The Position of Women" in the first edition of his *American Commonwealth,* 1888, he transfers from the article, almost word for word, the paragraph on mixed hunting parties in the Adirondacks. The book quickly became a classic. Abridged editions were issued. In these the paragraph on the Adirondacks is omitted, but it survived in the two-volume standard edition, reappearing in the revisions of 1893 and 1910 and in subsequent reprintings.

6. Harold Phelps Stokes is the author of a chapter of reminiscences on the St. Regis Yacht Club in the club book for the fiftieth anniversary, 1947.

7. A portage, for which wagons were once used, from the Upper St. Regis boat landing to Big Clear Pond (Lake Clear).

8. Five one-design classes of sailboats are used in competition on the St. Regis lakes. Of the Idems, Mr. John B. Trevor, Jr., of the St. Regis Yacht Club, writes in "Adirondack Sailors" (The *Ad-i-ron-dac,* July-August, 1960): "The 'Idem' class of one design sailboats was designed for these lakes by the naval architect Clinton Crane. By concentrating interest on identical boats, emphasized by the Latin name 'Idem,' the lake sailors were set on the path of perfecting their skills rather than trying to outbuild each other. These Idem boats still form the backbone of St. Regis sailboat racing; all twelve of the original Idems are still registered with the Club. It is possible that the Idems are the oldest one-design class in the world, in which the present class consists of all the original boats."

AFTERWORD

The following passages have been reproduced from a Camp Wild Air guest book. The camp, owned by Whitelaw Reid, Editor of the *New York Tribune* and Ambassador to the Court of St. James, was started for his niece and ward, Ella Reid. It is located on Upper St. Regis Lake, and the first cabin erected for her in 1882.

In 1903, Mr. Reid dictated to his secretary, Susan Strong, his recollections of early days on the lake. She wrote them down as shown in the guest book. Following her entry are names of guests who visited the camp in 1903 and 1904.

The camp is still thriving and is currently owned by Mr. Reid's grandson, also named Whitelaw Reid. His four children and seven grandchildren consider it about the greatest place there is.

WHITELAW REID
March 1992

Camp Wildair,
July 30th, 1903.

In 1881, Mr. Whitelaw Reid
sent his niece (+ ward) Miss Ella
Spencer Reid, to the Adirondacks
for her health, + she established
a day camp on Birch Island, then
unoccupied, where she remained
during the entire season. While
there she selected this spot for
a permanent camping ground
+ the next spring her guide,
Fred Barnes, put up here the first
permanent camp buildings on the
Upper St. Regis, — of which one,
"the little cabin", is still standing
+ in use. — She named the place
"Camp Wildair", occupied it during
the whole season of 1882, +

continued to return year by year,
either with her Uncle & family or
alone, till her removal to California.
Dr. Trudeau was then in Camp
on Spitfire; but there was no
other permanent camp on the
Upper St. Regis until Mr. White
(son-in-law of John D. Townsend)
established one where the Rev. Mr
Smith is now. Next came Dr.
Gautier at what is now the
Penfold Camp & Charles M. Lea
at the Garrett Camp. Then came
the Misses Parkins on the site of
the late Schlesinger Camp, now divided between Dr. James & Col. Peabody; & then the Anson Phelps
Stokes on Birch Island.

June 11th 1893 - Chauncey M. Depew.
July 12   Wm Rutherford Mead.

July 19th Louise Floyd Wickham

1903.
July 30th   Camp opened.

"   Whitelaw Reid.

"   Elisabeth Mills Reid

"   Ogden M. Reid

.   Jean Templeton Reid —

Aug. 7th   Moses Taylor —

"   Edith B. Taylor.

"   Moses Taylor Jr.

"   Reginald Bishop Taylor.

"   Francis Taylor

"   Marion Taylor.

"   Achel N Barney

" 8th   D. O. Mills

    Oliver B. Harriman

" 11th   Minto.   Government House. Ottawa

             Minto House
             Hawick.
" "   Mary Minto   Scotland

" "   Eileen Elliot

" "   Ruby Elliot.

1903.

15th Aug: Eleanor Roosevelt.
14 Aug. James E. Miller
15 Aug. Martha McCook.

Aug 17   Wm. D. Sloane.   2 W 52nd St NY
                            Lenox Mass
          Emily T. V. Sloane

Aug 17   J. Bowen Lee   New York
          D. O. Mills   do

Aug 18   Frederic Byers   Pittsburgh Pa.

Aug 30   John A. Dix.   New York.

Sept 3rd Elsie M. Nicholas Babylon L.I.

   10   Thomas Bailey Aldrich Boston
Sept 10   Lilian Aldrich
          Louise Aldrich

Sept 12   Francis Burton Harrison New York
          E. H. Harriman   Arden N.Y.
    "   Mary W. Harriman   "
    "   Mary Harriman   "

1904 Camp opened
1st Aug. Whitelaw Reid

" " Elisabeth Mills Reid

" " Jean Templeton Reid

3 " " M. Reid

2 August Anna Russell Cowles

" " W. Sheffield Cowles Jr.

" " _____ _____ _____

_____ _____ Leslie _ Macdonough

_____ Joseph M. Macdonough

15th August Emily Jay

" Augustus Jay

" " Emily J. V. Sloane

_____ _____

_____ _____

Aug 19 William Crozier   Washing_____

" " Wm B. Boulton, Jr.   Oien_____

" 20 W. H. Moody   Man'ts

" " Fred H Gillett   ..

21 Anna Russell Cowles   Farmington

[illegible]

" 26 Harry & Nicholas   New York
" 28 Elizabeth F. Harriman   Newport
" 30 Oliver B. Harriman   N.Y.

Sep. 1st Emily Margaret Gordon Dix   New York —
" 2d Thaddeus R. Snively, Chicago.

[illegible] Barnes   *[illegible]*
Sept 7 Beatrix Hoyt — Westchester

Sept 7th Russell E. Sard   Albany

           Ogden L. Mills
           E. H. Harriman   Arden
           Mary Harriman

Sept 15th Tillie H. Mortimer — Long Island
" " Stanley Mortimer.   Roslyn. L.I

Sept. 19th 1904.

           Camp Closed for the
           season.

house parties
typical day pg 50
best place — want to share it
  types of guests

caretaker: "go to play keeping log cabins"
types of guests